First World War
and Army of Occupation
War Diary
France, Belgium and Germany

47 DIVISION
141 Infantry Brigade,
Brigade Trench Mortar Battery
12 June 1916 - 31 August 1916

WO95/2739/2

The Naval & Military Press Ltd
www.nmarchive.com
Published in association with The National Archives

Published by

The Naval & Military Press Ltd

Unit 10 Ridgewood Industrial Park,
Uckfield, East Sussex,
TN22 5QE England
Tel: +44 (0) 1825 749494

www.naval-military-press.com

www.nmarchive.com

This diary has been reprinted in facsimile from the original. Any imperfections are inevitably reproduced and the quality may fall short of modern type and cartographic standards.

© **Crown Copyright**
Images reproduced by permission of The National Archives, London, England, 2015.

Contents

Document type	Place/Title	Date From	Date To
Heading	WO95/2739/2		
Heading	47th Division 141st Infy Bde 141st Lt Trench Mortar Bty Jun-Aug 1916		
Heading	141st Brigade 47th Division 141st Light Trench Mortar Battery June 1916		
War Diary	Angres Sector	12/06/1916	30/06/1916
Heading	141st Brigade 47th Division 141st Light Trench Mortar Battery July 1916		
War Diary	Angres Sector	01/07/1916	06/07/1916
War Diary	Souchez Sector	07/07/1916	28/07/1916
War Diary	Divion	29/07/1916	30/07/1916
War Diary	Monts En Ternois	31/07/1916	31/07/1916
Heading	141st Brigade 47th Division 141st Light Trench Mortar Battery August 1916		
War Diary	Monts En Ternois	01/08/1916	01/08/1916
War Diary	Fortel	02/08/1916	04/08/1916
War Diary	Acquet	05/08/1916	05/08/1916
War Diary	Novelles En Chaussee	06/08/1916	20/08/1916
War Diary	Famechon	21/08/1916	21/08/1916
War Diary	Havernas	22/08/1916	22/08/1916
War Diary	Molliens Au Bois	23/08/1916	23/08/1916
War Diary	Bresle	23/08/1916	31/08/1916

WO 95/27392

47TH DIVISION
141ST INFY BDE

141ST LT TRENCH MORTAR BTY
JUN - AUG 1916

141st Brigade.
47th Division.

141st LIGHT TRENCH MORTAR BATTERY.

JUNE 1916

141st Brigade.
47th Division.

Army Form C. 2118.

WAR DIARY
or
INTELLIGENCE SUMMARY.
(Erase heading not required.)

141 st Trench Mortar Battery

Vol 1 - 2 Y

Place	Date	Hour	Summary of Events and Information	Remarks and references to Appendices
Angre	12/6/16		141 and 141's Light Mortar Bty amalgamated and formed 141st TMBty as instructed in letter GHQ O/B B.166 dated 3rd March. Officers with unit Captain R.W.M'Crerkeny, Lt. S.H.N. EAMES, 2Lt. J.H. GELL, 2Lt. G.B. LOVELL	
-do-	13/6/16		Relieved 24th Bde TMBty at Railway Dugout. Casualties nil	
-do-	14/6/16		Enemy strafed with TM and rifle grenades. Retaliation by our mortars effective. Casualties nil	
-do-	15/6/16		2Lt. N.H. SMITH reported for duty. Casualties nil	
-do	15/6/16		Quiet day. Casualties nil	
-do-	16/6/16		Quiet day. Casualties nil	
-do-	17/6/16		Replied to enemy TM and RG activity. Relieved by 142nd TMBattery. Moved to billets at Scase 10. Casualties nil	
-do-	18/6/16		In Divisional reserve at Scase 10. Light training. Casualties nil	
-do-	19/6/16		In Divisional reserve at Scase 10. Light training. Casualties nil	
-do-	20/6/16		In reserve at Scase 10. Light training. Casualties nil	
-do-	21/6/16		Relieved 142nd TMBty. Replied to enemy TM fire. Casualties nil	
-do	22/6/16		Quiet day. Casualties nil	

Army Form C. 2118.

WAR DIARY
or
INTELLIGENCE SUMMARY.
(Erase heading not required.)

Instructions regarding War Diaries and Intelligence Summaries are contained in F.S. Regs, Part II. and the Staff Manual respectively. Title pages will be prepared in manuscript.

141st Trench Mortar Battery

Place	Date	Hour	Summary of Events and Information	Remarks and references to Appendices
Angre Dic	23/6/16		Quiet day. Casualties nil	
-do-	24/6/16		100 grenades with rifling T.M.G on strafe. Wire cutting. Casualties nil	
-do-	25/6/16		Strafe. Wire cutting continued. Reporting of M.G emplacements. Casualties nil	
-do-	26/6/16		Strafe. Wire cutting continued. Reporting of M.G. emplacements. Enemy active. Casualties nil	
-do-	27/6/16		Enemy quiet til 11.30 p.m. continued firing in support of raid by 19th Batt. Lon. Regt.	
-do-	28/6/16		Operations in support of 19th Batt. Lon. Regt. raid continued. Casualties 1 officer wounded 1 OR wounded. 2/Lt E.B. LATHAM 17th Batt Lon Regt. TURNER P.H. 17th Batt Lon Regt. 3779 bgs.	※
-do-	29/6/16		Repairing emplacements damaged by enemy's artillery fire. Casualties Nil	
-do-	30/6/16		Quiet day. Casualties Nil	

S.W. Lawson

141wt Brigade.
47th Division.

141st LIGHT TRENCH MORTAR BATTERY.

JULY 1 9 1 6 :P:::

141 TM Bty

Vol 2

WAR DIARY
INTELLIGENCE SUMMARY

Army Form C. 2118.

(Erase heading not required.)

Instructions regarding War Diaries and Intelligence Summaries are contained in F.S. Regs., Part II. and the Staff Manual respectively. Title pages will be prepared in manuscript.

Place	Date	Hour	Summary of Events and Information	Remarks and references to Appendices
Angres Sector	1/7/16		Trench mortar activity on both sides. Casualties NIL	
-do-	2/7/16		Enemy active. Trench mortar strafe. Repairing positions damaged by enemy's artillery fire. Casualties NIL	
-do-	3/7/16		Relieved by 142nd Trench Mortar Bty. Marched to billets at Fosse 10. Casualties NIL	
-do-	4/7/16		In Divisional reserve at Fosse 10. Physical drill bayonet fighting and also Battery Drill. Casualties NIL	
-do-	5/7/16		In Divisional reserve at Fosse 10. Physical drill bayonet fighting and Battery drill. Casualties nil	
-do-	6/7/16		In Div. reserve at Fosse 10. Physical drill bayonet fighting also Battery drill. Casualties NIL	
Loucher Sector	7/7/16		Relieved 140 TMB. Hqrs AIX NOULETTE. Casualties NIL	
-do-	8/7/16		2pm trench mortar support to raid by 142 BDE in ANGRES SECTOR. Casualties NIL	
-do-	9/7/16		Replied to enemy's artillery + trench mortar fire. Casualties NIL	
-do-	10/7/16		Quiet day. Casualties NIL	
-do-	11/7/16		Quiet day. Casualties NIL	
-do-	12/7/16		Quiet day. Casualties NIL	
-do-	13/7/16		Carried on diet with evacuation of positions	

Army Form C. 2118.

WAR DIARY
or
INTELLIGENCE SUMMARY.
(Erase heading not required.)

Instructions regarding War Diaries and Intelligence Summaries are contained in F. S. Regs., Part II. and the Staff Manual respectively. Title pages will be prepared in manuscript.

Place	Date	Hour	Summary of Events and Information	Remarks and references to Appendices
Louches Secteur	14/7/16		Enemy active with T/Mortars. Reply by us effective. Casualties NIL	
-do-	15/7/16		Aircraft artillery in evening. Fire T/ retaliation of enemy trench mortars. Casualties NIL	
-do-	16/7/16		Aircraft by artillery in day & evening of enemy wire. Casualties NIL	
-do-	17/7/16		1am. Raid by 20th Batt. Som. Regt. Enemy retaliation slight. Casualties 3 O.R. Pte. SLOPER J. 1st Batt. Som. Regt. Pte. MARDON 19th Batt Som. Regt.	
-do-	18/7/16		Retaliation on enemy's TM and RG aircraft in day by Heavy Artillery. Casualties NIL	
-do-	19/7/16		Quiet Day. Casualties NIL	
-do-	20/7/16		Relieved by 2nd NAVAL BDE TM/Bty. Moved to billets at Forae 10. Casualties NIL	
-do-	21/7/16		In Div reserve. B Light training. Casualties NIL	
-do-	22/7/16		In Div reserve. to R.N. Division. Light training. Casualties NIL	
-do-	23/7/16		In Div reserve to R.N. Div. Light training. Casualties NIL	
-do-	24/7/16		In Div reserve to R.N. Div. Light training. Casualties NIL	
-do-	25/7/16		In Div reserve to R.N. Div. Light Training. Casualties NIL	
-do-	26/7/16		In Div reserve to R.N. Div. Light Training. Casualties NIL	
-do-	27/7/16		Moved by forced march to new area as IV Corps Reserve. Casualties NIL	
-do-	28/7/16		Typical sub Heavy fighting. Saucy area. Casualties NIL	

WAR DIARY
or
INTELLIGENCE SUMMARY.

Army Form C. 2118.

Place	Date	Hour	Summary of Events and Information	Remarks and references to Appendices
DIVION	29/7/16		Prepared small bayonet fighting drawing ditch. Inspection of Rallery by Brig Gen. 141st. Bde at 2pm	
-do-	30/7/16		Moved by route marches to new area at MONT EN TERNOIS. Billeting party in advance. Move	
MONTS EN TERNOIS	31/7/16		completed at 1pm. Marching out state 5 Off. 60 OR. Marching in state 5 Off. 60 OR. Divine Service. Quiet day. Casualties Nil.	

[signature]

141st Brigade.
47th Division.

141st LIGHT TRENCH MORTAR BATTERY

AUGUST 1 9 1 6

WAR DIARY
INTELLIGENCE SUMMARY

14 I T M Bty

Vol 3

Place	Date	Hour	Summary of Events and Information	Remarks and references to Appendices
MONTS EN TERNOIS	1/8/16		Advance 2 miles for new area FORTEL. Jany Transport and also STM & OR's were complete by 1pm. Billeting accommodation very poor. Remainder in Bivouac.	
FORTEL	2/8/16		Received BM 251. In action below to ADMS at ROELINS or BONNIERS or Gun Park. Quiet day. Casualties NIL	
-do-	3/8/16		Received BM 355. Div Cavalry to reconnoitre an inland line with whom we shall be training to be carried out between 5am & 9am. Replies to Received BM 357. Guns were silent.	
-do-	4/8/16		Advance of route 5.45 am for new area ACQUET. Billeting reconnaissance party.	
ACQUET	5/8/16		Column of route began to move to new area NOYELLES-EN-CHAUSSÉE. Billeting accommodation fair.	
NOYELLES EN CHAUSSÉE	6/8/16		Training –. Physical drill bayonet fighting in new area. Received BM 285	
			Cancelling BM 285	
-do-	7-8-16		Training – Physical drill bayonet fighting musketry drill lecture on care of gun.	
-do-	8-8-16		Training – Physical drill bayonet fighting rifle drill musketry firing.	
-do-	9-8-16		Training – Physical drill bayonet fighting rifle drill & as training area.	
			Preparing gun positions for Brigade scheme	

Army Form C. 2118.

WAR DIARY
or
INTELLIGENCE SUMMARY.
(Erase heading not required.)

Place	Date	Hour	Summary of Events and Information	Remarks and references to Appendices
NOYELLES	10/8/16		Training - Company drill, bayonet fighting, box respirator drill, preparing & stripping for Brigade exercise.	
EN CHAUSSEE	11/8/16		Training - Company drill, bayonet fighting, box respirator drill & instruction.	
-do-	12/8/16		Training - Company drill, bayonet fighting. Carried out Brigade exercise to 10/96 (see attached)	
-do-	13/8/16		S.R.	
-do-	13/8/16		Rifle drill, musketry, jumping, bayonet drill.	
-do-	14/8/16		Training - Stand-to given in 00-108	
-do-	15/8/16		Divine Service in Bois de Creqy	
-do-	16/8/16		Repetition of exercise on night of 12/13. Bn. at 4.30 am	
-do-	17/8/16		Training - Bayonet drill, bombing, drill alarms & rifle fighting	
-do-	18/8/16		Bayonet drill. Route march with band. Rifle & instruction. Lewis Gun	
-do-	19/8/16		Training - Bayonet drill. Route march by sections	
-do-	20/8/16		Column of Route known to Rendezvous area FANECHON. Move completed 7pm. Billeting good.	
FANECHON	21/8/16		Column of Route known Bivouac area HAVERNAS. Move completed 6.30pm. Billeting good.	
HAVERNAS	22/8/16		Column of Route known area MOLLIENS AU BOIS. Move completed 10.30am. Billeting very poor.	
MOLLIENS AU BOIS	23/8/16		Column of Route to move bivouac area BRESLE. Move completed 1pm. Billeting poor. Commencing	

Army Form C. 2118.

WAR DIARY
or
INTELLIGENCE SUMMARY.
(Erase heading not required.)

Instructions regarding War Diaries and Intelligence Summaries are contained in F.S. Regs., Part II. and the Staff Manual respectively. Title pages will be prepared in manuscript.

Place	Date	Hour	Summary of Events and Information	Remarks and references to Appendices
BRESLE	23/8/16	7.45 pm	Practising night attacks + consolidating positions gained	
-do-	24/8/16		Minute inspection by O/C Battn. Received BM 502	
-do-	25/8/16		Physical drill, Musketry, dress inspection by OC Battn	
-do-	26/8/16		Inspects Drill - Battery drill	
-do-	27/8/16		Church parade - trekking parade	
-do-	28/8/16		Inspects drill - Battery drill	
-do-	29/8/16		Physical drill, Musketry Ammunition firing practise	
-do-	30/8/16		Quiet day owing to bad weather. Received BM 636. 42nd Brigade will hold pass rules on Sandpry pass. Received BM 77 & 78	
-do-	31/8/16		Brigade Exercise as given in OO 114. Received BM 550 & 551. Also OO 115	

S.W. Brandt
Lt Col
Cmdg

www.ingramcontent.com/pod-product-compliance
Lightning Source LLC
Chambersburg PA
CBHW081617160426

43191CB00011B/2167